children
of the DAY

1 & 2
Thessalonians

BETH MOORE

Leader Guide

LifeWay Press®
Nashville, Tennessee

Misty Brazell

Published by LifeWay Press®. © 2014 Beth Moore

ISBN 978-1-4300-3225-0 • Item 005644874

Dewey Decimal Classification: 227.1
Subject Headings: BIBLE. N.T. THESSALONIANS—STUDY \ CHRISTIAN LIFE \SPIRITUAL LIFE—GROWTH

Unless otherwise noted, all Scripture quotations are taken from the Holman Christian Standard Bible®, Copyright © 1999, 2000, 2002, 2003, 2009 by Holman Bible Publishers. Used by permission. Holman Christian Standard Bible®, Holman CSB®, and HCSB® are federally registered trademarks of Holman Bible Publishers. Scripture quotations marked NIV are from the Holy Bible, New International Version, copyright © 1973, 1978, 1984 by International Bible Society.

To order additional copies of this resource, write to LifeWay Church Resources Customer Service; One LifeWay Plaza; Nashville, TN 37234-0113; fax 615.251.5933; phone toll free 800.458.2772; email customerservice@lifeway.com; order online at www.lifeway.com; or visit the LifeWay Christian Store serving you.

Printed in the United States of America

Adult Ministry Publishing, LifeWay Church Resources, One LifeWay Plaza, Nashville, TN 37234-0152

About the Author

BETHANY McSHURLEY is a freelance editor/writer who specializes in Christian curriculum, autobiographies, and new-author development. Through both her work and ministry involvement at Long Hollow Baptist, she hopes to spread the message that a relationship with Jesus can radically transform every aspect of life. Bethany resides in Tennessee with her husband, Jon, and two sons, Aidan and Tristan.

Introduction

Children of the Day: 1 and 2 Thessalonians sheds light on the relationship shared by those who comprise the church. Together we stand shoulder-to-shoulder as we look outward, living in obedience to God's Word and in anticipation of Christ's coming. This guide will help you lead a study of *Children of the Day* for groups in your church or community. This guide provides helps for planning and promoting the study and instructions for conducting nine group-study sessions.

Course Overview

This in-depth course is designed to be completed over nine weeks through a combination of daily individual study and weekly group sessions.

INDIVIDUAL STUDY. Each participant needs a copy of the *Children of the Day* member book. The member book contains video viewer guides for nine sessions along with eight weeks of personal study. Every week contains five daily lessons, each requiring 30–45 minutes to complete at home in preparation for weekly group sessions.

GROUP SESSIONS. Participants meet once a week for a two-hour group session that encourages discussion and application of what they learned during their daily study. The small group encourages accountability and allows members to benefit from other participants' insights as they process the material studied. It also builds a sense of community.

Small groups help encourage relationships as participants share and pray together. In the large-group time, members watch video presentations in which Beth enhances the material in the book with additional truths and challenges.

Group-Session Format

For members to receive the greatest benefit from this study, plan for a weekly two-hour group session, plus a short check-in period. The most basic approach is to simply watch the video and use the related viewer guide and weekly questions to generate discussion. Following the fuller plan, however, provides members with intimate daily time with God through their workbook content, support and fellowship through small-group discussion and activity, and inspiration through video presentations. This guide's suggestions reflect the following schedule (times are arbitrary).

8:45 a.m.	Child care open, leaders ready (15 min. before session begins)
9:00 a.m.	Small groups (50 min.)
9:50 a.m.	Break and transition to large group (10 min.)
10:00 a.m.	Large group (65 min.)
	• Watch video sessions (60 min.)
	• Closing assignments and prayer (5 min.)
11:05 a.m.	Dismiss

Feel free to adjust schedule as needed. We encourage you not to omit three key things:

1. individual study of the member book at home
2. small-group discussion of option 1 (principal questions and personal discussion questions) or option 2 (growth and reflection activities)
3. viewing of the video sessions.

Optional Format

The ideal format for *Children of the Day* is a group-study time of two hours per week for a total of nine weeks; however, you may need another option to fit your group. Although many groups study these materials with an alternate schedule, members risk not getting into the habit of daily Bible study. In the introduction to the member book you will find the four-level option unique to *Children of the Day.* Adjust your time and schedule to fit the level that most of your participants choose.

If you adopt an alternate plan, encourage members to study the Bible daily. If your group can meet for only one hour a week, view the video one week and conduct small-group study the next. To maintain individual daily study, encourage members to complete the member book work during the first week and review it during the second week.

Included with the video content for this study is Priscilla Shirer's interview with Beth Moore. You may choose to watch it prior to the introductory session.

Resources

The following resources are also available:

· *Children of the Day: 1 and 2 Thessalonians* (member book) provides eight weeks of daily biblical study and viewer guides for nine sessions. Each participant needs a copy. Order item 005600950.
· *Children of the Day: 1 and 2 Thessalonians Leader Kit* contains one member book; this leader guide; and DVDs featuring nine video teaching sessions and bonus materials. Order item 005558691.
· *Children of the Day: 1 and 2 Thessalonians Audio CD Collection* includes audio portions of Beth's video presentations and printable listening guides. They are designed for individual study, but a leader may also wish to use them for personal review and inspiration. Order item 005644875.
• Audio and video downloads are available from *www.lifeway.com/childrenoftheday.*

Choosing Leaders

The following are descriptions of the responsibilities of leaders.

LARGE-GROUP LEADER. An organizer, coordinator, and facilitator who
• provides administrative leadership for the group
• schedules the study
• promotes and coordinates enrollment efforts
• enlists, coordinates, and supports small-group facilitators
• orders and distributes resources
• maintains and submits accurate records
• leads large-group video presentations and related closing each week

The large-group leader should be one who explores the crucial truths of God's Word and desires to help others grow. A heart prepared by God—being available and teachable—is more important than years of experience. Her success depends on a strong commitment to study and a faithful fulfillment of responsible group leadership.

SMALL-GROUP FACILITATORS. Enlist one facilitator for every 10–12 participants. These are not teachers but facilitators of discussion and fellowship. This study requires they also serve as community builders, working to make participants feel valued and connected. They are responsible to
- greet/register members at the introductory session
- contact group members after the introductory session to introduce themselves and give the location of the meeting room, providing participants with a point of contact by way of a phone number or email address.
- check attendance prior to each week's meeting (optional)
- take prayer requests, conduct prayer time at the start of small group, pray for members, and encourage participants to pray for one another
- guide members to discuss option 1 questions, to participate in the activities suggested for option 2, or to present a blend of both
- promote fellowship among group members
- note opportunities for follow-up ministry

If you have 12 or fewer participants, one facilitator can serve as both large- and small-group leader. This guide designates when small-group discussion is to occur. Each facilitator should note the following list of responsibilities, information, and tips.

Facilitating Small-Group Discussion
Small-group facilitators guide discussions of each week's homework using option 1 principal questions and personal discussion questions) or option 2 (growth and reflection activities). These are listed in this leader guide. Small-group facilitators can use the following guidelines to make discussion times effective, to challenge participants spiritually, and to promote life change:
- Make seating arrangements inclusive, so participants can see each other.
- In your first meeting, provide participants with your phone number or email address. Be open to mentoring opportunities.
- Greet members as they arrive. Start on time. Share prayer requests and pray (5 min.). Make notes as requests are shared. Encourage members to pray for one another during the week. If someone is experiencing difficult circumstances, send a note or call between sessions to say that you are praying for her and that you care. Be willing to be a friend to those in your small group.
- Use the remainder of your small-group time to address the questions outlined in option 1 or the activities in option 2. Adapt and change the questions as necessary. Be flexible if members wish to spend more time on one group of questions or if they raise specific issues. Encourage and lead participants to share insights about their weekly homework.

Promoting the Study

Social media, church bulletins, newsletters, handouts, posters, announcements in worship services and Sunday school classes, and word of mouth are excellent ways to promote the study. Sometimes local radio and television stations will announce upcoming events free of charge. The "Promotional Video" segment in the kit can help publicize the study [1:00].

In "4 Levels of Doing This Study" [2:50], Beth further explains the four levels of study. You may choose to share it with small-group leaders prior to your first session or use it to present the concept during the introductory meeting. While this leader guide provides ideas for incorporating all levels, women are encouraged to choose the degree of participation that best meets their needs. Please discourage competition.

Session 1
BACKGROUND OF 1 & 2 THESSALONIANS

Introduction

This two-hour introduction to *Children of the Day: 1 and 2 Thessalonians* is designed as a large-group session and will introduce the Sunburst, an after-meeting activity geared toward building relationship with the Lord and/or with others. Please read through the entire session prior to meeting.

Objectives

In this session you will complete the following:
- Register all participants and assign registrants to their small groups.
- Welcome all participants; explain format basics and participation levels.
- Familiarize attendees with the topic of living in community as children of the day.
- Watch session 1.
- (Optional) view Beth's recitation of the Books of Thessalonians [16:15].

Before the Session

1. ENLIST SMALL-GROUP LEADERS for groups of no more than 12. Briefly meet prior to the introductory session and watch Beth's "Message to Leaders" [6:00]. Discuss the information on pages 5–6 and emphasize the need to smile and warmly greet participants as they arrive each week. Seek to foster a sense of community.

2. WORK WITH OTHERS TO BRAINSTORM ways to use the concept of crepuscular rays (the visible columns of sunshine that stream through gaps in the clouds) when decorating your meeting space. Discuss musical selections sharing a "light" theme that can be played as participants enter the common area. Ideas include "We Are" (by Kari Jobe), "Shine, Jesus, Shine," "Go Light Your World," "In the Light," and "Here I Am to Worship." Work as a team to create and supply props and decorations. Should you expect more than 25 participants, arrange registration tables at the common meeting room's entrance. Label registrar stations with A–F, G–L, M–R, and S–Z to represent the first letter of participants' last names. Consider designating those each leader registers as members of her group. Adjust as needed and avoid cliques.

3. ASK EACH LEADER TO WEAR A NAME TAG and to be at her station a half hour before registration begins. Prepare her to specifically thank participants for coming and to tell them that she is glad they chose to attend. Supply member books, registration forms (you prepare), pens, name tags, and goody bags if desired.

4. **MAKE SURE THE VISUAL AID FOR THE FIRST SUNBURST IS IN PLACE:** Two armchairs should be placed at the front of your meeting area, facing one another as if inviting a heart-to-heart conversation. Place a box of tissues and a Bible on a small table between the two chairs. Leave yourself space to maneuver around them.

5. **SET UP VIDEO EQUIPMENT** to view session 1 and the optional recitation.

During the Session

1. **ASK PARTICIPANTS TO REGISTER** at the table representing the first letter of their last names. Strive to make eye contact, smile, and warmly greet each participant as she arrives. The goal is to make participants feel valued and included.

2. **BEGIN WITH PRAYER.** Welcome participants and introduce the leadership. If the total number of those gathered equals less than 20, allow time for participant introductions.

3. **READ ALOUD 1 JOHN 1:5-7 AND 1 THESSALONIANS 5:5.** Say, *Sometimes it seems like our common enemy, the Devil, is gaining ground in this world. But we must not forget that the Lord Jesus is the ultimate victor, and He has placed us on earth as His ambassadors. Over the next weeks, we are going to learn how to join together as a body of believers, living as children of the day who press back against the Enemy's darkness. We'll let the Lord invade the shadowy places of our hearts and grow us in fellowship with one another.*

4. **PRESENT INSTRUCTIONS** regarding the format of the course.
    a) Using either Beth's "4 Levels of Doing This Study" video or pages 7–9 of the member book, introduce the involvement levels. Stress that participants should choose the level that best meets their needs rather than succumbing to the temptation to feel as though it's a contest.
    b) Encourage participants to flip through their member books, asking them to complete week 1 homework for next week. Note that all subsequent sessions will begin in the small-group meeting areas. If necessary, explain that group leaders will touch base with participants during the week to give room assignments.
    c) Suggest participants begin their study by reading the introduction (member book, p. 10–11).
    d) Emphasize the benefits of small-group interaction, which will
        • reinforce basic biblical truths presented;
        • help form ideas for how to apply what is learned; and
        • build camaraderie and support among friends sharing a journey.

5. **ENCOURAGE TIME AWARENESS** in the small groups. Classes should begin promptly, and comments should stay on topic.

6. **POINT OUT THE VIEWER GUIDE** on page 12–13 of the member book. The answers are on p. 24 of this leader guide and also online. Show session 1 [59:00].

Closing

1. **STAND BEHIND** the two chairs and table you set up prior to the meeting. Place one hand on each chair and say, *Some of us came to this session unsure whether we really wanted to commit to this Bible study. Life's not been going so well. We've been nursing hurts. Shutting people out. Shutting God out. But I want you to know that you are here for a reason, and it's time to let go of whatever it is you are carrying. The Lord wants you to release whatever has a hold on your heart so that you might walk like the child of His light that you are.*

2. **ASSIGN THE FIRST SUNBURST.** Sit in one of the two chairs and say, *This week—before you even think about opening your member book—sit down for a heart-to-heart with God. Pull up a chair just for Him, and tell Him about your hurts. Ask Him to set you free. Invite the Lord to teach you about Himself and choose to live in the expectation that He will.*

3. **PRAY AND DISMISS.**

After the Session

1. **MEET WITH REGISTRARS** and adjust small-group size as needed.

2. **ASK A VOLUNTEER** to create an attendance sheet for each small-group leader.

3. **ENCOURAGE LEADERS TO CONTACT EACH WOMAN** in their small group via email or text to thank them for their interest in the study and inform them of their small group's meeting location.

4. **MAKE SURE EACH LEADER HAS A COPY OF THE LEADER GUIDE** and encourage leaders to review the suggested questions and activities well before the next meeting. Remind them that the option 2 growth and reflection activities, should they choose to incorporate them, may require preparation.

Session 2
THE LORD'S MESSAGE RANG OUT

Before the Session
Choose whether to pursue option 1, 2, or a blend of both with your small group. Be aware that the growth and reflection activities may require supplies and prep time.

Small Groups
Give a warm welcome. To facilitate introductions, ask those present to turn to page 36 in their member book. Encourage each participant to share her name as well as one specific characteristic that helps to distinguish her taste, learning style, or personality from that of her family and friends. Begin by sharing your own.

OPTION 1: Discuss the week's principal and personal discussion questions. The short version of the questions appear on the viewer guide to aid group discussion. The page numbers point to the questions in the member book.

● Principal Questions
DAY 1: Over how many Sabbaths did they serve in Thessalonica? (p. 16)
DAY 2: Who wrote each letter to the Thessalonians? (p. 19)
DAY 3: How, according to Paul, did the gospel come to the Thessalonians? (p. 25)
DAY 4: The Thessalonian believers "became" what two things (1 Thess. 1:6-7)? (p. 28)
DAY 5: What sounded forth from the Thessalonians after their conversion? (p. 32)

○ Personal Discussion Questions
DAY 1: How are you impacted by the knowledge that the Holy Spirit had you in mind as Scripture was penned? (p. 18)
DAY 2: What good memory do you have from a harsh season of your life? (p. 20)
DAY 3: How would you describe the Holy Spirit within you bearing witness? (p. 24)
DAY 4: Do you embrace or struggle with the fact our God is filled with joy? (p. 28)
DAY 5: Describe a situation in which you witnessed or participated in "the excited transmission" of the gospel. (p. 34)

OPTION 2: Growth and Reflection Activities
1. PRESENT A GLOBE or world map and identify modern Thessaloniki, Greece. Explain that the first-century Christians, like those in Thessalonica, as well as those gathered here today are all a part of the church. Point out that Genesis 11:1-8 explains how God divided the languages and scattered humanity, paving the way for the diversity we see

and hear. Read aloud Revelation 7:9-10. Ask, *How can this picture of diverse believers unified in heaven influence the way we view Christians of other cultures and times? Why is this important to our study?*

2. **GIVE EACH PARTICIPANT** an eight-inch section of yarn. Ask them to gently test its strength before separating the fibers into individual strands and again testing for endurance. Discuss how this visual illustrates the truth that Christians "have an intrinsic need to be part of a team." Ask, *What do we gain by partnering with other believers?*

3. **SHARE ABOUT** a time when someone served as Christ's love-in-action for you, noting ways her outreach strengthened your faith. Then read through the following examples before asking participants to identify how such shows of support could build trust in the Lord's love and interest.
   - Missy's Sunday school leader offers to babysit her kids free of charge.
   - Ruth Ann's friend stays late after a church event to help her pack up leftovers and clear tables.
   - A nursery worker welcomes Angie's new baby by bringing a pack of diapers and a homemade pie to her door.
   - A woman in Gayle's small group texts her a favorite Scripture verse and a smile.

4. **PASS OUT CONSTRUCTION PAPER AND MARKERS.** Challenge participants to see themselves as messengers of the gospel. Say, *With the Holy Spirit's help, we can participate in taking God's Word to our communities and beyond.* Then instruct participants to "map" their own spheres of influence, listing people and places that they might feasibly reach with the gospel of Christ. Provide copies of the sample on page 25 to get them started.

Use the last moments to share insights from your maps and to address questions. Close the time with prayer.

Large Group

Show session 2 [60:00]. Refer participants to pages 36–37 in their member books to fill in the viewer guide (answers on p. 24).

Announce Sunburst: Ask participants to stand and link arms across the aisles of your meeting area. Say, *Whether you see yourself as a* we, you, *or* they, *you are part of the church, Christ's bride. And Sister Loved by God, I know He has chosen you!*

Together, let's look outward this week. Before our next session, take the time to come alongside someone new to your church family or community. Though we stand shoulder-to-shoulder here, there are many ladies outside this group—many of them believers or seekers—who feel lonely and cut off from hope. Make it your goal to be the active love of Jesus at work in someone's life over the course of these next days. You just might gain a new friend.

Session 3
ENTRUSTED WITH THE GOSPEL

Small Groups

Welcome participants. Encourage them to share how they loved on someone for the Lord this week. Affirm those who participated and encourage all present to be on the lookout for ways to reach out to the disconnected.

OPTION 1: Discuss the week's principal and personal discussion questions.

● Principal Questions

DAY 1: What happened to Paul and Silas after they were dragged into the marketplace before the authorities? (p. 39)

DAY 2: What two gifts might believers share with those to whom they minister? (p. 44)

DAY 3: What action verb is used in 1 Thessalonians 2:12 and 4:1 (ESV) to describe how we journey with God? (p. 47)

DAY 4: How had the Thessalonians become "imitators of God's churches in Christ Jesus that are in Judea"? (p. 51)

DAY 5: In 1 Thessalonians 2:19-20, what words did Paul use to describe the Thessalonian Christians? (p. 58)

○ Personal Discussion Questions

DAY 1: What do you think God is searching out and testing our hearts to find? (p. 41)

DAY 2: If 1 Thessalonians 2:8 stirred up a story in you, share it with your group. (p. 46)

DAY 3: How does Christ walking among the churches encourage you? (p. 49)

DAY 4: Share a time when you experienced some form of persecution because of your belief in Jesus. (p. 51)

DAY 5: Have you ever avoided relationships to avoid pain? (p. 59)

OPTION 2: Growth and Reflection Activities

1. ENCOURAGE PARTICIPANTS TO SHARE about any blessings they've enjoyed this week as they embraced or applied the phrase, "Sister Loved by God, I know He has chosen you!" Ask, *What does the idea that we are sisters in the Lord mean to you?*

2. SAY, *Paul spoke about sharing his life with the Thessalonians.* Hold up each of the following items, asking how they might apply to sharing our lives with those in our circles: a photo album, a clock, a box of tissues, a Bible, a coffee cup. Working as a group, describe what "sharing our lives" could look like. Ask, *What purpose could this serve to the world? Within the body of Christ?*

3. **ON DAY 5, BETH FOCUSED ON THE NEED FOR COMMUNITY** among believers. Discuss ways we in the church might unintentionally leave someone feeling "orphaned." Create a list of indicators that might suggest a sister in the Lord is feeling disconnected. Commit to looking for those signs in the coming week, seeking God's guidance in how to draw those sisters into a greater sense of connectivity.

4. **DISTRIBUTE COPIES OF THE WORKSHEET ON P. 26.** Explain that "Susan Eversobusy" isn't sure she has time to invest in a younger sister in the faith. Assume she has requested the group's advice in finding ways to make outreach and encouragement a part of her week. Working together, address the worksheet. Note aloud that this activity is not meant to criticize how an individual spends her day; instead, it is an exercise in learning to think creatively about finding time for others.

Use the last five minutes of either small-group option to address questions and comments. Close the small-group time with prayer.

Large Group

Show session 3 [60:00]. Refer participants to the viewer guide on page 60–61 in their member book.

Announce Sunburst: Say, *Our first task this week is to go back to that place where we met with the Lord after session 1. We can ask Him to parent us, to reveal and address what would draw us closer in our relationship with Him.*

After that, we must look outward again. We need to seek out a younger sister in the Lord whom we might help through mentoring. Pray about it, and when God lays someone on your heart, send her a note that tells her you are praying for her and shows your willingness to connect with her regularly. Make a purposeful effort to convey your availability and then put the outcome in the Lord's hands.

- not getting a call back when sign up to volunteer

- not saying "hi" when you're a greeter

- existing cliques

- when people say "Oh, is this your 1st time?"

Session 4
DESTINED FOR THIS

Small Groups

Welcome participants and then write the word "hindrances" on a poster or tear sheet at the front of the room. As a group, define the term. See page 63 in the member book if you need help.

OPTION 1: Discuss the week's principal and personal discussion questions.

● Principal Questions

DAY 1: What was Satan seeking to prevent by keeping the missionaries and the Thessalonians apart? (p. 65)

DAY 2: How did Paul go about proclaiming the kingdom of God and teaching things concerning the Lord Jesus Christ? (p. 69)

DAY 3: What was Timothy sent to Thessalonica to do? (p. 72)

DAY 4: By what did Paul not want the Thessalonians to be moved? (p. 77)

DAY 5: What profound change in prayer language is introduced in 1 Thessalonians 3:11? (p. 81)

○ Personal Discussion Questions

DAY 1: See the Human Hindrance Spectrum on page 65. What examples did you give to illustrate the dangers of "legalism" and "license"? (p. 65)

DAY 2: Which of the equations on pages 70–71 spoke to you? Explain. (p. 71)

DAY 3: Describe a time when you felt all your planning had flown the coop, leaving you to just react. (p. 76)

DAY 4: What maladies come to mind at the mention of the word "affliction"? (p. 77)

DAY 5: What does the possibility that Paul may have dictated at least some of his letters through Silas contribute to your understanding of their relationship? (p. 83)

OPTION 2: Growth and Reflection Activities

1. **SAY,** *Knowing one's enemy can help in determining defensive measures. To better identify hindrances the Devil uses to deter us from connecting with others and reaching our full ministry potential, imagine you can listen in on a strategy meeting. What suggestions might be posed to …*
   - Keep Jean and Kelly from witnessing outside the downtown women's clinic?
   - Prevent Emily from being kind to a girl with a colorful reputation?
   - Discourage Vicki from believing for her husband's salvation?
   - Deter the women's ministry from starting a program to feed the homeless?

2. **AS A GROUP, LOOK AT THE EQUATIONS ON PAGES 70–71.** Ask, *What new perspective did you gain on your hindrances as you read through these equations?*

3. **FLOAT A TOY SAILBOAT** in a long, shallow pan. Gently blow against the sail so that the boat moves forward. Then request a show of hands regarding how many have ever wanted to give up because sailing through life was not so smooth. Remind participants that Paul and Silas faced incredible hardships, and the writing of Thessalonians highlights the fact that things rarely went according to their plans. Still, "God was ever at the helm," of their circumstances (p. 76, member book). Ask, *How can this reminder help you when life gets stormy* [rock the pan] *and you want to give up?*

4. **PASS OUT INDEX CARDS AND PENS** before reading Romans 8:18, 28-39 and Hebrews 10:35-36 aloud. Ask participants to listen for assurances that our afflictions are never wasted. Encourage each of them to write Romans 8:37 on an index card.

Large Group

Show session 4 [58:30]. Refer participants to page 86 in their member books.

Announce Sunburst: Say, *Some of us have become bogged down by hindrances, frustrated with our situations, and irritated with the very people God placed in our lives that we might love them toward Him. Daughter, maybe your mother tries your patience. Mentor, maybe the young woman you wanted to invest in dismissed your first attempt and embarrassed you. Perhaps your coworker is so prickly that it's all you can do to be polite to her. This week, ask God to help you love in the midst of a troubled relationship. Actively put your heart out there in whatever way He reveals. This week, love someone in spite of herself. That's how God loves us.*

Session 5
TAUGHT BY GOD

Small Groups

Welcome participants. Invite them to share a favorite insight from their study so far.

OPTION 1: Discuss the week's principal and personal discussion questions.

● Principal Questions

DAY 1: What kind of life did Christ say He'd come to give in John 10:10? (p. 90)

DAY 2: Exactly why did the Thessalonians have no need for anyone to write to them about brotherly love? (p. 94)

DAY 3: What two reasons did Paul give in 1 Thessalonians 4:12 for the directives he issued in verse 11? (p. 98)

DAY 4: What group of people has the first access at the coming of the Lord? (p. 103)

DAY 5: Compare Exodus 19:16-20 and 1 Thessalonians 4:16-18. (p. 107)

○ Personal Discussion Questions

DAY 1: How does the phrase "more and more" contradict the notion of a place of arrival in this earthly journey in which we simply maintain from there? (p. 90)

DAY 2: Share about someone who learned biblical truth straight from God, apart from textbook, training, or a human teacher. (p. 97)

DAY 3: What is the most prominent lesson you have had to learn about minding your own business? (p. 101)

DAY 4: What might be gained through thinking of death in terms of sleep? (p. 104)

DAY 5: What are you most curious about concerning end-time events? (p. 106)

OPTION 2: Growth and Reflection Activities

1. **GIVE A MEASURING TAPE** to two participants. Have them stand and slowly extend the tape between them. Say, *This week we learned that love, humility, boldness in evangelism, and rejoicing can grow "more and more." But what simultaneously shrinks in our lives when they do?* Have participants sit down and then hold up a sand-filled timer to visually represent growth and decrease. Turn it upside down and ask, *What must decrease in me as my love increases?* (hate; cynicism) *What must decrease as my rejoicing increases?* (dissatisfaction, criticism) *My boldness in evangelizing?* (fear, awkwardness)

2. **NOTE ALOUD** that we live in an upside-down world where overt sensuality and selfish manipulation are culturally acceptable, making them seem less than dangerous. Ask, *But how can we respond when we overhear one of our Christian sisters say, "I don't care what they think. I'm going to do what I want"?*

3. **DISCUSS** whether it is more comforting to think of a deceased believing friend as having died or having fallen asleep. Explain your reasoning.

4. **ASK FOR A VOLUNTEER** to read Revelation 21:1-4,22-26 aloud. Explain that this is a glimpse into heaven. Say, *Beth referred to Christ's return as a whole new era of "Let there be Light." What do you think she meant by that?* (See also Gen. 1:1.)

Close the small-group time with prayer.

Large Group

Show session 5 [64:00]. Refer participants to pages 110-111 in their member book.

Announce Sunburst: Say, *Sisters, we are a community of women on a journey to holiness. Whether you need to make changes in the physical department or in your reading material or television preferences, seek God's input in the matter of your sexual purity. Even if you feel the 28-Day Challenge doesn't apply to you, please ask the Lord to search your heart on this topic and pray that He might help you grow in holiness. Do not allow sexual sin—or any other hang-up—to be the Enemy's secret weapon in crippling your walk with Christ.*

Session 6
CHILDREN OF LIGHT

Small Groups
OPTION 1: Discuss the week's principal and personal discussion questions.

● Principal Questions
DAY 1: Exactly what will come "like a thief in the night"? (p. 116)
DAY 2: What two pieces of attire do children of the day "put on"? (p. 122)
DAY 3: What words or concepts pop into your mind when you hear "wrath"? (p. 123)
DAY 4: To whom are the responsibilities in 1 Thessalonians 5:14-15 assigned? (p. 132)
DAY 5: How should a believer pray? What does "pray constantly" mean? (p. 136)

○ Personal Discussion Questions
DAY 1: What part of your experience fights to distort your biblical beliefs? (p. 115)
DAY 2: What one event in your life shook you to your most awakened state? (p. 121)
DAY 3: How does God's wrath differ from ours? (p. 126)
DAY 4: What is an admonition you accepted and a reason you're glad you did? (p. 131)
DAY 5: Which of the exhortations in 1 Thessalonians 5:16-22 do you need most to apply in your present circumstances? (p. 135)

OPTION 2: Growth and Reflection Activities
1. ASK FOR A VOLUNTEER to read Genesis 6:11-13 aloud. As a group, discuss parallels between this scene just before the flood and our current age. Read aloud and then discuss the related significance of 2 Peter 3:8-10.
2. REFER TO *THE HOBBIT* EXCERPT on page 122. Identify the adventure God calls us to in this age where darkness has taken up residence in our land. Ask, *How do we become distracted by "doilies" and "dishes"? What is the danger of doing so?*
3. HAVE THREE VOLUNTEERS STAND in the outer edges of the room and assign the following parts: Karen, Joy, and Consuelo. Note that Christians often feel like tiny islands scattered over the ocean of humanity. Linked, we are transformed into a tightly woven net of community. Hold up an inflated swim ring tied to a long length of rope. Say, *First Thessalonians 5:14-15 explains that Christians should warn, comfort, and help one another. How might I warn, comfort, or help each of the ladies in the following situations?**
   - Karen's once-regular church attendance has slowed to a crawl, and her small group was cancelled last week because she didn't show up to lead it.
   - Joy tells me she's just not in love with her husband anymore and plans to divorce him.
   - Consuelo has lost much of her physical mobility after a car accident, and I can see that she's in pain, though she never says anything about it.

*As suggestions are offered, apply the ideas to Karen, Joy, and Consuelo. As you do, toss the life ring to each of them. Tug your end of the rope to draw each woman back into the circle of church community. Explain your actions.

4. DISCUSS how warnings can be gifts of loving grace.

Large Group

Show the video for session 6 [63:30]. Refer to page 138–139 of member books.

Announce Sunburst: Note aloud that we can trust God's Word as the authority on every subject it touches. Say, *Isn't it a blessing to know that Scripture is not just for Bible teachers or preachers or missionaries, but for every believer? We really can own and live out its truths!* Read aloud 1 Thessalonians 5:13b-14. Encourage participants to put that passage into practice this week, pursuing what is good for those in the family of God.

Session 7
MOBILIZED MINISTRY

Before the Session

Large-group leader, for this week's Sunburst you will need a large clock with a visible second hand. See below for more information.

Small Groups

Ask participants to share about how they worked to do what is good in their interactions with the family of God this week. Warmly affirm their efforts.

OPTION 1: Discuss the week's principal and personal discussion questions.

● Principal Questions

DAY 1: What exhortation is recorded in Colossians 4:17? (p. 142)

DAY 2: What answered prayer do you see reflected in 1 Thess. 3:12 and 2 Thess. 1:3? (p. 146)

DAY 3: What did God tell the prophet Ezekiel to do before he spoke to Israel? (p. 150)

DAY 4: How did Paul describe the symbiosis between a believer's effort and Christ's involvement in Colossians 1:29? (p. 157)

DAY 5: Who is in charge of providing what we need to do God's will? (p. 158)

⭕ Personal Discussion Questions

DAY 1: Have other's contributions encouraged or discouraged you lately? Explain. (p. 144)

DAY 2: How has God used others to encourage, train, or direct you? (p. 149)

DAY 3: Would you like to share your letter on what Scripture means to you? (p. 153)

DAY 4: In what task could you use some equipping from the Scriptures? (p. 155)

DAY 5: God's equipping can take the form of *preparing* or *repairing.* How are the two distinct? (p. 159)

OPTION 2: Growth and Reflection Activities

1. **SAY,** *Your ministry is the ever-accruing collection of your life works for the glory of God* (p. 138). Ask each participant to identify one part of the ministry God has assigned her in this season. After each response, ask, *What specific gift or ability has the Lord given you to fulfill your role?* Affirm answers.

2. **HAVE PARTICIPANTS TAKE TURNS** sharing ways that others have proved strategic to their spiritual development. Draw attention to the variety of responses: grandmothers and coworkers can be just as influential as pastors and Sunday school teachers when it comes to encouraging others in their walk with the Lord.

3. **INTRODUCE A TWELVE-INCH FASHION DOLL AS "NANCY."** Explain that Nancy oversees her corporation's charity giving, is raising three foster kids, and strives to live out her sincere Christian faith. When asked where she attends church, however, Nancy always replies, "I spend my Sundays out in the sunshine." Ask, *How might you lovingly convince Nancy to rethink church? Why is it important that she does?*

4. **AS A GROUP, CONSIDER WILLIAM TYNDALE'S STORY** (p. 151–153). Encourage participants to summarize his ministry and explain how his life's work impacts them. Ask, *Does it change your perspective to think of William as your brother in Christ? Explain.*

Use the last five minutes to address questions. Close with prayer.

Large Group

Show the video for session 7 [60:00]. Refer to pages 162–163 in member books.

Announce Sunburst: Hold up a battery-powered clock, preferably one on which the second hand's movement can be clearly seen by participants. Say, *In only a little while, Jesus Christ will be revealed. Every moment of our lives, then, has the potential to make a difference for eternity. The message that God sent His Son to save all who would believe in Him is the most important truth we can share, but are we sharing it?*

This week, tell somebody about Jesus Christ. Whether in person or by letter, whether to someone in your immediate circle, or someone you meet at the post office, use the moments God has given you to share His truth. You, Sister Loved by God, are His witness to the world.

Session 8
TO LOVE THE TRUTH

Before the Session

Large-group leader, for this week's activities you will need to make copies of the handouts on pages 27 and 28. Ideally, for page 28, you'll provide each participant with a copy of the handout as well as an envelope. See below for more information.

Small Groups

OPTION 1: Discuss the week's principal and personal discussion questions.

● Principal Questions

DAY 1: What three potential sources of alarm did Paul list in 2 Thessalonians 2:2? (p. 166)
DAY 2: What specific events occur before the Day of the Lord (2 Thess. 2:1-7)? (p. 171)
DAY 3: What characteristic of the spirit of the antichrist is in 1 John 4:2-3? (p. 176)
DAY 4: Based on 2 Thessalonians 2:9-12 alone, why are people perishing? (p. 182)
DAY 5: Based on 2 Thessalonians 2:15, what did Paul tell the Thessalonians to stand firm and hold onto? (p. 186)

○ Personal Discussion Questions

DAY 1: Have you ever been duped by someone who proved to be an imposter? (p. 168)
DAY 2: What will you be thankful to find missing in Christ's coming kingdom? (p. 172)
DAY 3: Which historical rulers might qualify as types of antichrists? (p. 175)
DAY 4: What do you think any process of sifting can be meant to accomplish? (p. 180)
DAY 5: What do you think it means to keep yourself in the love of God? (p. 185)

OPTION 2: Growth and Reflection Activities

1. BETH TAUGHT, "THE SINGULAR GUARD AGAINST DECEPTION IS TRUTH."
   Ask participants to read and cut apart the Scripture guard towers copied from page 27. Then read aloud the following list of deceptions related to the end times. Participants should respond to each statement by holding up the tower displaying a biblical truth that would protect them from believing each specific lie. Ask a volunteer to read the related verse aloud in each instance.
   - Deception 1: Christ returned many years ago. We missed it. (See 2 Thess 2:1-3.)
   - Deception 2: The Messiah is currently living in a Middle Eastern village. We must join him there. (See Matt 24:23-24, 26-27.)
   - Deception 3: Mark your calendar—Christ will return on January 18, 2080. (See Matt 24:36,44.) Emphasize the need to remain in Scripture daily, thus growing less susceptible to deceptive ideas and philosophies.

2. **ASK FOR A VOLUNTEER TO DRAW** on a poster or tear sheet two masculine silhouettes representing Judas Iscariot and the Antichrist. Compare and contrast the two, discussing the roles they play in the story of Scripture. (See day 2 and day 3 for help.) Note aloud that God's purposes are accomplished in spite of evil. Praise Him for that truth.

3. **SAY,** *Just as Satan tries to use human rebellion to his advantage, he intends to manipulate the circumstances of our lives to pull us off the course of following God.* Display a mesh strainer, a bowl, and a can of grated Parmesan cheese. (For best results, expose the cheese to air overnight.) Slowly pour the cheese into the strainer and gently shake it over the bowl. Note aloud that as we wait for Christ's return, we may be sifted by an enemy bent on our destruction. Ask, *But what might sifting accomplish from God's viewpoint?* (See p. 180.) Point out that the sifted cheese represents "strengthened faith." Encourage participants to identify what the remaining lumps might represent (doubt, fear, anger, half-heartedness, bad habits, etc.).

4. **POINT OUT** that crepuscular rays, columns of sunlight breaking through the clouds, are used throughout the artwork for this study. Say, *This week's session was heavy with information about the Enemy's schemes and the rise of darkness. But with what beautiful light of truth did day 5's content pierce the darkness?*

Close the small group time with prayer, using 2 Thessalonians 2:16-17 as a benediction.

Large Group

Show the video for session 8 [59:30]. Refer participants to pages 188–189 in their member books to fill in the viewer guide (answers on p. 24).

Announce Sunburst: Say, *As you leave today, remember that in this time leading to Christ's coming, He is actively working through you and me to reach the world. Our number one job is to tell people the good news of Christ. This week we are going to make a specific effort to reach those who are strangers to us—though the Lord knows their stories.*

Pass out copies of the activity on page 28 as well as envelopes suited to size. Fold each copy in half to make a card. Encourage each participant to purchase a $15 gas card to place in the envelope along with the card, which should be addressed with the word "Friend." Sealed envelopes should be placed on the windshields of parked cars throughout the community.

Close by praying for God's guidance in knowing where each card should be placed.

Session 9
THE LORD OF PEACE

Before the Session
Large-group leader, please provide one permanent marker and one marble for each participant. They will be used during this week's video session.

Small Groups
Begin by asking participants to share about ways this study has deepened their sense of the church as a community or developed their identity as children of the day.

OPTION 1: Discuss the week's principal and personal discussion questions.

● Principal Questions
DAY 1: What do 1 Thessalonians 5:25 and 2 Thessalonians 3:1 have in common? (p. 191)

DAY 2: What things are of most importance (1 Cor. 15:1-4)? (p. 198)

DAY 3: What command had Paul and his coworkers given the Thessalonians when they were still with them? (p. 199)

DAY 4: By what title is God called in 2 Thessalonians 3:16? (p. 205)

DAY 5: What thread embroiders together each greeting and benediction? (p. 208)

○ Personal Discussion Questions
DAY 1: Is the idea of receiving rather than achieving a shift for you or have you practiced this approach for years? (p. 194)

DAY 2: What are a few specific places you desire for the words of Christ that abide in you to arrive with you over the next month? (p. 198)

DAY 3: What is a destructive attitude you've seen go viral among believers? (p. 202)

DAY 4: Share about a time when you fought depression and despair and asked God why certain events were permitted on your path. (p. 204)

DAY 5: What are some of the things going through your head on this final day? (p. 207)

OPTION 2: Growth and Reflection Activities
1. ASK PARTICIPANTS TO RAISE THEIR HANDS if they have ever struggled with the feeling that God is bothered or annoyed when they approach Him in prayer. Point out that Ephesians 3:12 teaches that through faith in Jesus we may approach God with freedom and with confidence. Note that while it is totally appropriate to clasp hands in prayer, humbly requesting God's help, we go to Him as daughters much-loved by our Father—who does not need us to beg. Ask, *How might going to the Lord with your palms open and lifted change your prayer life?*

2. **NOTE THAT FOR HUNDREDS OF YEARS** Scripture was copied by hand, translated, and shared by Christians who were often persecuted because of their faithfulness to the gospel mission. Ask participants to hold their Bibles close to their hearts and close their eyes. As a group, sit in silence for a moment, meditating on the fact that the torch of sharing God's Word has passed to us. Ask, *What will you do with the fact that YOU are tasked with sharing this precious gospel with the world?*

3. **NOTE THAT CONTROVERSIES AND DIVISIONS** among those within the church take our eyes off the mission of sharing the gospel. As a group, discuss how best to diffuse the following situation:

   • You meet for coffee with three ladies from your choir and one of them asks if you've noticed how dull the Sunday services have become lately. "Nobody is getting spiritually fed around here anymore," another sighs. Ask, *What impact might your response, or lack thereof, have on the health of your local church?*

4. **ENCOURAGE PARTICIPANTS TO SET THEIR ALARMS** to take in a sunrise this week. Ask them to treasure it as a visual reminder that the Son will return and forever obliterate the Enemy's darkness. Our Prince of Peace will come, and we, Sisters Loved by God, will forever live in the light of His victory.

Large Group

Show the video for session 9 [65:00]. Refer participants to pages 212–213 in their member books to fill in the viewer guide.

Announce Sunburst: Pass one marble to each participant. Say, *We as the church in this time and place have been given the Word of God and a mission to share the good news of Jesus Christ. As we wrap up our time together, please place this marble in your pocket or purse. Let it travel with you each day as an ongoing reminder that you've got the ball; YOU are the bearer of God's good news to the world. Let His Word influence your interactions with your sisters in the Lord. Let Him change the way you relate to those in your home. Let Him work through you to call others to His side.*

Close in prayer and with the exhortation, "The grace of our Lord Jesus Christ be with you all."

Viewer Guide Answers

SESSION 1
Paul; Silvanus; Timothy
1. gap ripped open; severed relationship
2. same edge; sharpen; slice
3. next person; meet; dearest
4. gone awry; frame; mind taught; God

SESSION 2
first drops; inspired ink; pen
1. WE; YOU; THEY; WE; Effectual; YOU; Affecting; THEY; Affected; 100 names
2. WE; YOU; you; loved; chosen
3. God; work; get; know
4. pretense; platforms; prove ourselves; proved
5. can see us; can see them
6. Jesus comes; keep coming

SESSION 3
whole parenting; no-holes parenting
1. Nurtured
2. Affectionately Desired
3. Accepting; Very Self
4. Exhorted
5. Encouraged
6. Charged; Walk Worthy

SESSION 4
1. entitlement; unbearable; vulnerable; wound; physically wounded; attack; damage
2. high-cost investment

3. illusion; control
1. pure reciprocity
2. sheer relief
3. coloring; memory
4. coming alive; unrestrainable madness; love

SESSION 5
sexual ethics; limitations; sexual conduct; no limitations; sexual conduct
1. pertinent now; then; *porneía*
2. doable; you; doing
3. learnable; each; learn
4. honorable; require; honor

SESSION 6
quench; Spirit; despise prophecies; word; Lord; direct prompting; clearness; energy; authority; speaking; God's name; extracurricular word; Scripture; strengthening; encouragement; comfort; legitimate; extracurricular; incomplete; must; tested; eliminate; examine; abused; correcting abuse; commanding disuse; abuse; use; lazy; Spirit-led

SESSION 7
Lord Jesus; revealed; Revelation; unveiling; grander; interpretation; glorious; temporarily residing abroad;

1. Now
2. little while
3. revealed
revealed; Relief; come; afflicted; *anesin;* Eternal relocation; Marveling; glorified; saints

SESSION 8
1. mystery; lawlessness; secret power
2. active restraint; lawlessness; something; someone; pressure; person; Holy Spirit; church; Paul; gospel; Rome/the Emperor; empire; state
1. restrainer; out; way
2. rebellion; come
3. man; lawlessness; *apocalypto; parousia;* parody; anti-*parousia;* Go; proclaim; gospel; deceivers; gone; world
1. dawn; appearance
2. kill; lawless; breath; nothing

SESSION 9
1. potent two-fold; prayer; speed ahead; honored; delivered; wicked; evil; drag along; drawing; oneself; rescuing; place; Without place; having no place; absurd; unreasonable; 10-Word; Upturn; not all; faith; Lord; faithful
2. personal signature; grace; with you all

THE WORD OF THE LORD
REACHES THROUGH ME

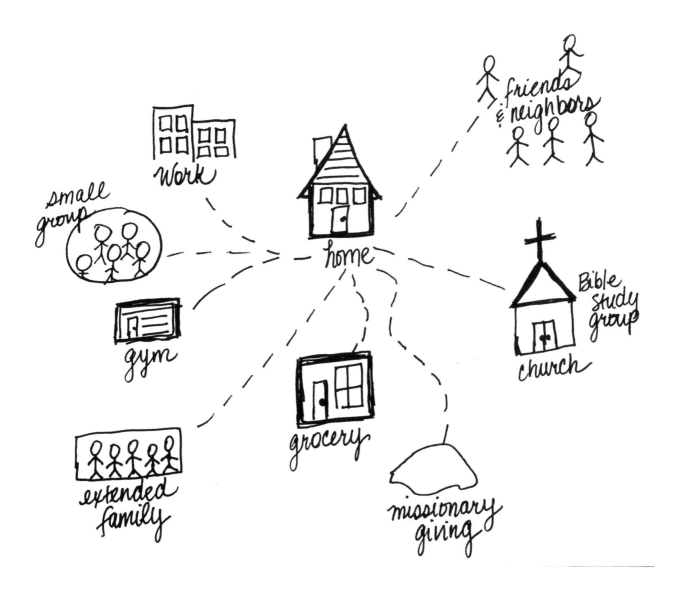

children
of the DAY

TOO BUSY?

Susan Eversobusy isn't sure she has the time to be a mentor. Assume she has requested your advice in finding ways to make outreach and encouragement a part of her day.

1. In the margin, affirm Susan in what she is doing well.
2. Place a star beside activities that might be abbreviated occasionally.
3. Circle activities that might be repurposed.
4. At the bottom of the page, list practical means of outreach and connection that she might weave into her day.

MONDAY

5:00 am	Wake up
5:00-5:30	Bible Study
5:30-6:30	Shower and Prep Time
6:30-7:00	Get Kids up and fed
7:00- 7:15	Family devotion time
7:15-8:00	Getting Kids to school and work commute
8:00-11:00	Work
11:00-12:00	Lunch at desk/Social media break
12:00-5:00	Work
5:00-5:15	Commute
5:15-6:30	Homework help/ dinner prep
6:30-7:00	Dinner
7:00-8:00	Household Chores
8:00-9:00	Crafting/Reading Time
9:00-10:30	Television

GUARD AGAINST DECEPTION

"Now concerning that day and hour no one knows—neither the angels in heaven, nor the Son—except the Father only ... This is why you also must be ready, because the Son of Man is coming at an hour you do not expect."

MATTHEW 24:36,44

"If anyone tells you then, 'Look, here is the Messiah!' or, 'Over here!' do not believe it! False messiahs and false prophets will arise and perform great signs and wonders to lead astray, if possible, even the elect ... So if they tell you, 'Look, He's in the wilderness!' don't go out; 'Look, He's in the inner rooms!' do not believe it. For as the lightning comes from the east and flashes as far as the west, so will be the coming of the Son of Man."

MATTHEW 24:23-24, 26-27

Now concerning the coming of our Lord Jesus Christ and our being gathered to Him: We ask you, brothers, not to be easily upset in mind or troubled, either by a spirit or by a message or by a letter as if from us, alleging that the Day of the Lord has come. Don't let anyone deceive you in any way. For that day will not come unless the apostasy comes first and the man of lawlessness is revealed, the son of destruction.

2 THESSALONIANS 2:1-3

A PERSONAL NOTE

Greetings!

I'm leaving you this gift today as
a reminder that God sees you.
He knows everything about you,
and He loves you dearly.

Please use this prepaid gas card
to fill your tank and allow the Bible
passage to fill your heart.

Blessings!

"For God so loved the world (including you!)
that he gave his one and only Son (Jesus Christ),
that whoever believes in him shall not perish
but have eternal life. For God did not send
his Son into the world to condemn the world,
but to save the world through him."
JOHN 3:16-17, NIV

LIVING PROOF LIVE

Bring your group to Living Proof Live with Beth Moore!

lifeway.com/livingproof

LifeWay Women | events

EVERYTHING IS BETTER WHEN SHARED

Have you noticed that women like to share good things with each other? We love to tell our friends when we get a great deal, find a new bakery in town, listen to an interesting podcast, or discover a useful parenting tip—we share just about anything that helps our sister in Christ on her journey. So, why not share a women's conference experience with your friends or your church group? It's so easy. Anyone with a willing heart can be a group leader. If you're already the one who makes things happen, sends the emails, and gathers your friends, this will be a breeze.

You have experienced the impact that the truth of God's Word can have. And you know that something special happens when we pull away from our everyday surroundings and give ourselves room to breathe. There are hurting women all around you, desperate for hope and peace. Help these women find that breathing room by creating this opportunity.

Try these tips when bringing a group to an event:

• Decide on an event location and date.

• Gather names of those you want to join you.

• Secure hotel rooms and transportation.

• Make sure everyone has registered for the event.

• Organize a meeting place and time to depart, and set up other necessary meet up times & locations.

• Collect cell phone numbers for everyone in your group.

• Think through weather conditions and meal options.

• Plan a couple activities for the drive home to help the ladies share their experiences.

• Schedule a Bible study after the event to keep women connected.

Find all the info you need to get started at lifeway.com/livingproof

Whatever we need, Jesus is.
Whatever we lack, Jesus has.
—Beth Moore

Experience Living Proof Live
lifeway.com/livingproof

LifeWay Women | events

YOU DID IT!

You've done a great job leading your group through the *Children of the Day* Bible study. If you enjoyed studying the Word with Beth Moore together, you'll love the experience of **LIVE Bible study** at an event near you or via simulcast. So gather your girls and get a Beth Moore event on your calendar today!

Visit lifeway.com/livingproof for dates, locations & details.

LifeWay Women | events